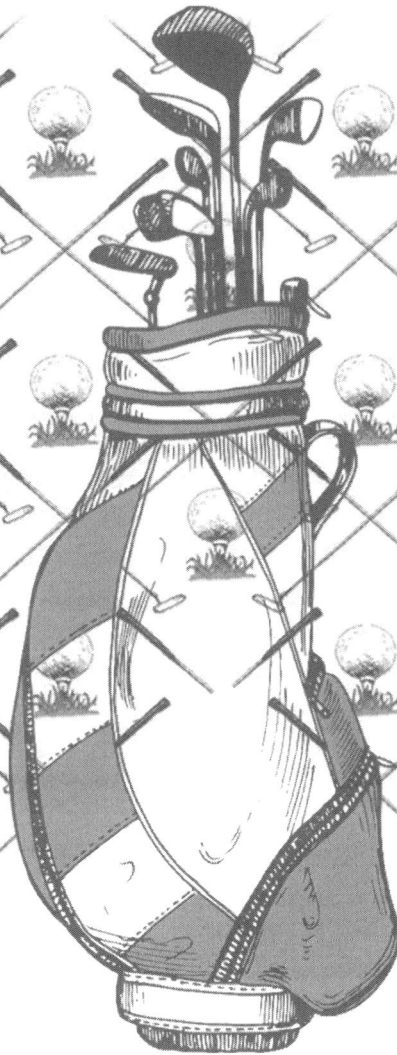

This Golf Journal Belongs To:

_____

COURSE
SCORECARDS
&
NOTES

GAME SCORES

Course:

Date: Tee Off Time:

Handicap: _____

Par: _____

Yardage: _____

Slope: _____

Rating: _____

Weather

Conditions: _____

Temperature: _____

Wind: _____

○ Casual

○ Competition

○ 9 Holes

○ 18 Holes

Players

_____

_____

_____

_____

Front 9

	1	2	3	4	5	6	7	8	9	TOTAL	GRAND TOTAL
PAR											
SCORE											
TEE BOX											
YARDAGE											
FW											
GIRs											
U&D											
PUTTS											
PENALTIES											

Back 9

	1	2	3	4	5	6	7	8	9	TOTAL	GRAND TOTAL
PAR											
SCORE											
TEE BOX											
YARDAGE											
FW											
GIRs											
U&D											
PUTTS											
PENALTIES											

My Score   Birdies   Doubles+   3-Putts+

Total Pars   Bogeys   Triples+   Penalties

MY YARDAGES

Date:

CLUB	HEAD WIND	TAIL WIND	NO WIND
Driver			
3-Wood			
3-Hybrid			
4-Hybrid			
5-Iron			
6-Iron			
7-Iron			
8-Iron			
9-Iron			
PW			
GW			
SW			
LW			

Notes from the 19th Hole

GAME SCORES

Course:

Date: Tee Off Time:

Weather

Conditions:

Temperature:

Wind:

Handicap:

Par:

Yardage:

Slope:

Rating:

Casual

Competition

9 Holes

18 Holes

Players

Front 9

	1	2	3	4	5	6	7	8	9	TOTAL	GRAND TOTAL
PAR											
SCORE											
TEE BOX											
YARDAGE											
FW											
GIRs											
U&D											
PUTTS											
PENALTIES											

Back 9

	1	2	3	4	5	6	7	8	9	TOTAL	GRAND TOTAL
PAR											
SCORE											
TEE BOX											
YARDAGE											
FW											
GIRs											
U&D											
PUTTS											
PENALTIES											

My Score   Birdies   Doubles+   3-Putts+

Total Pars   Bogeys   Triples+   Penalties

MY YARDAGES

Date:

CLUB	HEAD WIND	TAIL WIND	NO WIND
Driver			
3-Wood			
3-Hybrid			
4-Hybrid			
5-Iron			
6-Iron			
7-Iron			
8-Iron			
9-Iron			
PW			
GW			
SW			
LW			

Notes about this Course

Notes about my Performance

Notes from the 19th Hole

GAME SCORES

Course:

Date: Tee Off Time:

Handicap:

Par:

Yardage:

Slope:

Rating:

Weather

Conditions:

Temperature:

Wind:

Casual

Competition

9 Holes

18 Holes

Players

Front 9

	1	2	3	4	5	6	7	8	9	TOTAL	GRAND TOTAL
PAR											
SCORE											
TEE BOX											
YARDAGE											
FW											
GIRs											
U&D											
PUTTS											
PENALTIES											

Back 9

	1	2	3	4	5	6	7	8	9	TOTAL	GRAND TOTAL
PAR											
SCORE											
TEE BOX											
YARDAGE											
FW											
GIRs											
U&D											
PUTTS											
PENALTIES											

My Score   Birdies   Doubles+   3-Putts+

Total Pars   Bogeys   Triples+   Penalties

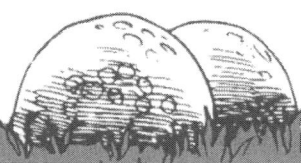

MY YARDAGES

Date:

CLUB	HEAD WIND	TAIL WIND	NO WIND
Driver			
3-Wood			
3-Hybrid			
4-Hybrid			
5-Iron			
6-Iron			
7-Iron			
8-Iron			
9-Iron			
PW			
GW			
SW			
LW			

Notes about this Course

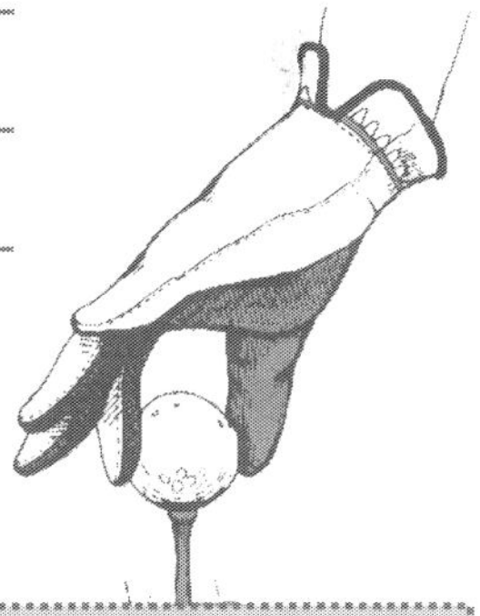

Notes about my Performance

Notes from the 19th Hole

GAME SCORES

Course:

Date:	Tee Off Time:

Weather

Conditions: _____

Temperature: _____

Wind: _____

Handicap: _____

Par: _____

Yardage: _____

Slope: _____

Rating: _____

○ Casual

○ Competition

○ 9 Holes

○ 18 Holes

Players

_____

_____

_____

_____

Front 9

	1	2	3	4	5	6	7	8	9	TOTAL	GRAND TOTAL
PAR											
SCORE											
TEE BOX											
YARDAGE											
FW											
GIRs											
U&D											
PUTTS											
PENALTIES											

Back 9

	1	2	3	4	5	6	7	8	9	TOTAL	GRAND TOTAL
PAR											
SCORE											
TEE BOX											
YARDAGE											
FW											
GIRs											
U&D											
PUTTS											
PENALTIES											

My Score   Birdies   Doubles+   3-Putts+

Total Pars   Bogeys   Triples+   Penalties

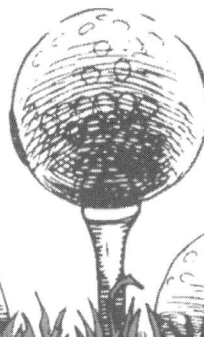

MY YARDAGES

Date:

CLUB	HEAD WIND	TAIL WIND	NO WIND
Driver			
3-Wood			
3-Hybrid			
4-Hybrid			
5-Iron			
6-Iron			
7-Iron			
8-Iron			
9-Iron			
PW			
GW			
SW			
LW			

Notes about this Course

Notes about my Performance

Notes from the 19th Hole

GAME SCORES

Course:

Date: Tee Off Time:

Handicap:
_____

Par:
_____

Yardage:
_____

Slope:
_____

Rating:
_____

Weather

Conditions:
_____

Temperature:
_____

Wind:
_____

○ Casual

○ Competition

○ 9 Holes

○ 18 Holes

Players

_____

_____

_____

_____

Front 9

	1	2	3	4	5	6	7	8	9	TOTAL	GRAND TOTAL
PAR											
SCORE											
TEE BOX											
YARDAGE											
FW											
GIRs											
U&D											
PUTTS											
PENALTIES											

Back 9

	1	2	3	4	5	6	7	8	9	TOTAL	GRAND TOTAL
PAR											
SCORE											
TEE BOX											
YARDAGE											
FW											
GIRs											
U&D											
PUTTS											
PENALTIES											

My Score   Birdies   Doubles+   3-Putts+

Total Pars   Bogeys   Triples+   Penalties

MY YARDAGES

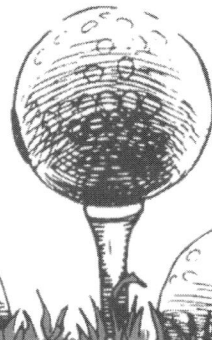

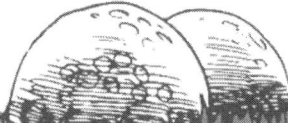
Date:

CLUB	HEAD WIND	TAIL WIND	NO WIND
Driver			
3-Wood			
3-Hybrid			
4-Hybrid			
5-Iron			
6-Iron			
7-Iron			
8-Iron			
9-Iron			
PW			
GW			
SW			
LW			

Notes about this Course

Notes about my Performance

Notes from the 19th Hole

GAME SCORES

Course:

Date: Tee Off Time:

Handicap:
_____

Par:
_____

Yardage:
_____

Slope:
_____

Rating:
_____

Weather

Conditions:
_____

Temperature:
_____

Wind:
_____

○ Casual

○ Competition

○ 9 Holes

○ 18 Holes

Players

_____

_____

_____

_____

Front 9

	1	2	3	4	5	6	7	8	9	TOTAL	GRAND TOTAL
PAR											
SCORE											
TEE BOX											
YARDAGE											
FW											
GIRs											
U&D											
PUTTS											
PENALTIES											

Back 9

	1	2	3	4	5	6	7	8	9	TOTAL	GRAND TOTAL
PAR											
SCORE											
TEE BOX											
YARDAGE											
FW											
GIRs											
U&D											
PUTTS											
PENALTIES											

My Score   Birdies   Doubles+   3-Putts+

Total Pars   Bogeys   Triples+   Penalties

MY YARDAGES

Date:

CLUB	HEAD WIND	TAIL WIND	NO WIND
Driver			
3-Wood			
3-Hybrid			
4-Hybrid			
5-Iron			
6-Iron			
7-Iron			
8-Iron			
9-Iron			
PW			
GW			
SW			
LW			

Notes about this Course

Notes about my Performance

Notes from the 19th Hole

GAME SCORES

Course:

Date: Tee Off Time:

Handicap:
_____

Par:
_____

Yardage:
_____

Slope:
_____

Rating:
_____

Weather

Conditions:
_____

Temperature:
_____

Wind:
_____

○ Casual

○ Competition

○ 9 Holes

○ 18 Holes

Players

_____

_____

_____

_____

Front 9

	1	2	3	4	5	6	7	8	9	TOTAL	GRAND TOTAL
PAR											
SCORE											
TEE BOX											
YARDAGE											
FW											
GIRs											
U&D											
PUTTS											
PENALTIES											

Back 9

	1	2	3	4	5	6	7	8	9	TOTAL	GRAND TOTAL
PAR											
SCORE											
TEE BOX											
YARDAGE											
FW											
GIRs											
U&D											
PUTTS											
PENALTIES											

My Score   Birdies   Doubles+   3-Putts+

Total Pars   Bogeys   Triples+   Penalties

MY YARDAGES

Date:

CLUB	HEAD WIND	TAIL WIND	NO WIND
Driver			
3-Wood			
3-Hybrid			
4-Hybrid			
5-Iron			
6-Iron			
7-Iron			
8-Iron			
9-Iron			
PW			
GW			
SW			
LW			

Notes about this Course

_____
_____
_____
_____
_____
_____
_____
_____

Notes about my Performance

_____
_____
_____
_____
_____
_____
_____
_____
_____
_____

Notes from the 19th Hole

GAME SCORES

Course:

Date: Tee Off Time:

Weather

Conditions: _____

Temperature: _____

Wind: _____

Handicap: _____

Par: _____

Yardage: _____

Slope: _____

Rating: _____

○ Casual

○ Competition

○ 9 Holes

○ 18 Holes

Players

_____

_____

_____

_____

Front 9

	1	2	3	4	5	6	7	8	9	TOTAL	GRAND TOTAL
PAR											
SCORE											
TEE BOX											
YARDAGE											
FW											
GIRs											
U&D											
PUTTS											
PENALTIES											

Back 9

	1	2	3	4	5	6	7	8	9	TOTAL	GRAND TOTAL
PAR											
SCORE											
TEE BOX											
YARDAGE											
FW											
GIRs											
U&D											
PUTTS											
PENALTIES											

My Score   Birdies   Doubles+   3-Putts+

Total Pars   Bogeys   Triples+   Penalties

MY YARDAGES

Date:

CLUB	HEAD WIND	TAIL WIND	NO WIND
Driver			
3-Wood			
3-Hybrid			
4-Hybrid			
5-Iron			
6-Iron			
7-Iron			
8-Iron			
9-Iron			
PW			
GW			
SW			
LW			

Notes about this Course

Notes about my Performance

GAME SCORES

Course:

Date: Tee Off Time:

Handicap: _____

Par: _____

Yardage: _____

Slope: _____

Rating: _____

Weather

Conditions: _____

Temperature: _____

Wind: _____

◯ Casual

◯ Competition

◯ 9 Holes

◯ 18 Holes

Players

_____

_____

_____

_____

Front 9

	1	2	3	4	5	6	7	8	9	TOTAL	GRAND TOTAL
PAR											
SCORE											
TEE BOX											
YARDAGE											
FW											
GIRs											
U&D											
PUTTS											
PENALTIES											

Back 9

	1	2	3	4	5	6	7	8	9	TOTAL	GRAND TOTAL
PAR											
SCORE											
TEE BOX											
YARDAGE											
FW											
GIRs											
U&D											
PUTTS											
PENALTIES											

My Score   Birdies   Doubles+   3-Putts+

Total Pars   Bogeys   Triples+   Penalties

MY YARDAGES

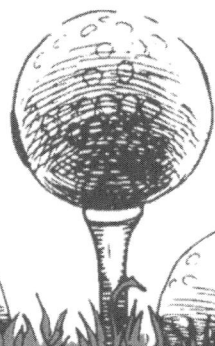

Date:

CLUB	HEAD WIND	TAIL WIND	NO WIND
Driver			
3-Wood			
3-Hybrid			
4-Hybrid			
5-Iron			
6-Iron			
7-Iron			
8-Iron			
9-Iron			
PW			
GW			
SW			
LW			

Notes about this Course

Notes about my Performance

Notes from the 19th Hole

GAME SCORES

Course:

Date:	Tee Off Time:

Handicap:
_____

Par:
_____

Yardage:
_____

Slope:
_____

Rating:
_____

Weather

Conditions:
_____

Temperature:
_____

Wind:
_____

- Casual
- Competition
- 9 Holes
- 18 Holes

Players

_____

_____

_____

_____

Front 9

	1	2	3	4	5	6	7	8	9	TOTAL	GRAND TOTAL
PAR											
SCORE											
TEE BOX											
YARDAGE											
FW											
GIRs											
U&D											
PUTTS											
PENALTIES											

Back 9

	1	2	3	4	5	6	7	8	9	TOTAL	GRAND TOTAL
PAR											
SCORE											
TEE BOX											
YARDAGE											
FW											
GIRs											
U&D											
PUTTS											
PENALTIES											

My Score   Birdies   Doubles+   3-Putts+

Total Pars   Bogeys   Triples+   Penalties

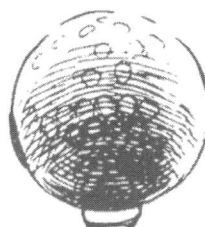

MY YARDAGES

Date:

CLUB	HEAD WIND	TAIL WIND	NO WIND
Driver			
3-Wood			
3-Hybrid			
4-Hybrid			
5-Iron			
6-Iron			
7-Iron			
8-Iron			
9-Iron			
PW			
GW			
SW			
LW			

Notes about this Course

Notes about my Performance

Notes from the 19th Hole

GAME SCORES

Course:

Date: Tee Off Time:

Handicap:
_____

Par:
_____

Yardage:
_____

Slope:
_____

Rating:
_____

Weather

Conditions:
_____

Temperature:
_____

Wind:
_____

○ Casual

○ Competition

○ 9 Holes

○ 18 Holes

Players

_____

_____

_____

_____

Front 9

	1	2	3	4	5	6	7	8	9	TOTAL	GRAND TOTAL
PAR											
SCORE											
TEE BOX											
YARDAGE											
FW											
GIRs											
U&D											
PUTTS											
PENALTIES											

Back 9

	1	2	3	4	5	6	7	8	9	TOTAL	GRAND TOTAL
PAR											
SCORE											
TEE BOX											
YARDAGE											
FW											
GIRs											
U&D											
PUTTS											
PENALTIES											

My Score   Birdies   Doubles+   3-Putts+

Total Pars   Bogeys   Triples+   Penalties

MY YARDAGES

Date:

CLUB	HEAD WIND	TAIL WIND	NO WIND
Driver			
3-Wood			
3-Hybrid			
4-Hybrid			
5-Iron			
6-Iron			
7-Iron			
8-Iron			
9-Iron			
PW			
GW			
SW			
LW			

Notes about this Course

Notes about my Performance

GAME SCORES

Course:

Date: Tee Off Time:

Handicap:
_____

Par:
_____

Yardage:
_____

Slope:
_____

Rating:
_____

Weather

Conditions:
_____

Temperature:
_____

Wind:
_____

Casual

Competition

9 Holes

18 Holes

Players

_____

_____

_____

_____

Front 9

	1	2	3	4	5	6	7	8	9	TOTAL	GRAND TOTAL
PAR											
SCORE											
TEE BOX											
YARDAGE											
FW											
GIRs											
U&D											
PUTTS											
PENALTIES											

Back 9

	1	2	3	4	5	6	7	8	9	TOTAL	GRAND TOTAL
PAR											
SCORE											
TEE BOX											
YARDAGE											
FW											
GIRs											
U&D											
PUTTS											
PENALTIES											

My Score   Birdies   Doubles+   3-Putts+

Total Pars   Bogeys   Triples+   Penalties

MY YARDAGES

Date:

CLUB	HEAD WIND	TAIL WIND	NO WIND
Driver			
3-Wood			
3-Hybrid			
4-Hybrid			
5-Iron			
6-Iron			
7-Iron			
8-Iron			
9-Iron			
PW			
GW			
SW			
LW			

Notes about this Course

Notes about my Performance

Notes from the 19th Hole

GAME SCORES

Course:

Date: | Tee Off Time:

Weather

Conditions:

Temperature:

Wind:

Handicap:

Par:

Yardage:

Slope:

Rating:

○ Casual

○ Competition

○ 9 Holes

○ 18 Holes

Players

Front 9

	1	2	3	4	5	6	7	8	9	TOTAL	GRAND TOTAL
PAR											
SCORE											
TEE BOX											
YARDAGE											
FW											
GIRs											
U&D											
PUTTS											
PENALTIES											

Back 9

	1	2	3	4	5	6	7	8	9	TOTAL	GRAND TOTAL
PAR											
SCORE											
TEE BOX											
YARDAGE											
FW											
GIRs											
U&D											
PUTTS											
PENALTIES											

My Score   Birdies   Doubles+   3-Putts+

Total Pars   Bogeys   Triples+   Penalties

MY YARDAGES

Date:

CLUB	HEAD WIND	TAIL WIND	NO WIND
Driver			
3-Wood			
3-Hybrid			
4-Hybrid			
5-Iron			
6-Iron			
7-Iron			
8-Iron			
9-Iron			
PW			
GW			
SW			
LW			

Notes about this Course

Notes about my Performance

Notes from the 19th Hole

GAME SCORES

Course:

Date:	Tee Off Time:

Weather

Conditions: _____

Temperature: _____

Wind: _____

Handicap: _____

Par: _____

Yardage: _____

Slope: _____

Rating: _____

○ Casual

○ Competition

○ 9 Holes

○ 18 Holes

Players

_____

_____

_____

_____

Front 9

	1	2	3	4	5	6	7	8	9	TOTAL	GRAND TOTAL
PAR											
SCORE											
TEE BOX											
YARDAGE											
FW											
GIRs											
U&D											
PUTTS											
PENALTIES											

Back 9

	1	2	3	4	5	6	7	8	9	TOTAL	GRAND TOTAL
PAR											
SCORE											
TEE BOX											
YARDAGE											
FW											
GIRs											
U&D											
PUTTS											
PENALTIES											

My Score   Birdies   Doubles+   3-Putts+

Total Pars   Bogeys   Triples+   Penalties

MY YARDAGES

Date:

CLUB	HEAD WIND	TAIL WIND	NO WIND
Driver			
3-Wood			
3-Hybrid			
4-Hybrid			
5-Iron			
6-Iron			
7-Iron			
8-Iron			
9-Iron			
PW			
GW			
SW			
LW			

Notes about this Course

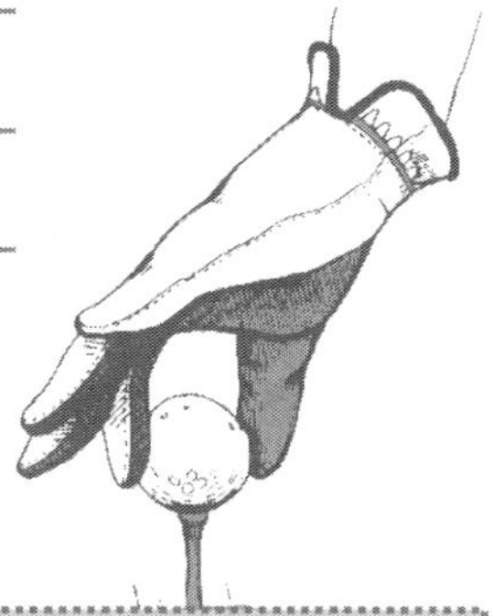

_____

_____

_____

_____

_____

_____

_____

Notes about my Performance

_____

_____

_____

_____

_____

_____

_____

_____

_____

Notes from the 19th Hole

GAME SCORES

Course:

Date: Tee Off Time:

Handicap:
_____

Par:
_____

Yardage:
_____

Slope:
_____

Rating:
_____

Weather

Conditions:
_____

Temperature:
_____

Wind:
_____

Casual

Competition

9 Holes

18 Holes

Players

_____

_____

_____

_____

Front 9

	1	2	3	4	5	6	7	8	9	TOTAL	GRAND TOTAL
PAR											
SCORE											
TEE BOX											
YARDAGE											
FW											
GIRs											
U&D											
PUTTS											
PENALTIES											

Back 9

	1	2	3	4	5	6	7	8	9	TOTAL	GRAND TOTAL
PAR											
SCORE											
TEE BOX											
YARDAGE											
FW											
GIRs											
U&D											
PUTTS											
PENALTIES											

My Score   Birdies   Doubles+   3-Putts+

Total Pars   Bogeys   Triples+   Penalties

MY YARDAGES

Date:

CLUB	HEAD WIND	TAIL WIND	NO WIND
Driver			
3-Wood			
3-Hybrid			
4-Hybrid			
5-Iron			
6-Iron			
7-Iron			
8-Iron			
9-Iron			
PW			
GW			
SW			
LW			

Notes about this Course

Notes about my Performance

Notes from the 19ᵗʰ Hole

GAME SCORES

Course:

Date: Tee Off Time:

Handicap:

Par:

Yardage:

Slope:

Rating:

Weather

Conditions:

Temperature:

Wind:

○ Casual

○ Competition

○ 9 Holes

○ 18 Holes

Players

_____

_____

_____

_____

Front 9

	1	2	3	4	5	6	7	8	9	TOTAL	GRAND TOTAL
PAR											
SCORE											
TEE BOX											
YARDAGE											
FW											
GIRs											
U&D											
PUTTS											
PENALTIES											

Back 9

	1	2	3	4	5	6	7	8	9	TOTAL	GRAND TOTAL
PAR											
SCORE											
TEE BOX											
YARDAGE											
FW											
GIRs											
U&D											
PUTTS											
PENALTIES											

My Score   Birdies   Doubles+   3-Putts+

Total Pars   Bogeys   Triples+   Penalties

MY YARDAGES

Date:

CLUB	HEAD WIND	TAIL WIND	NO WIND
Driver			
3-Wood			
3-Hybrid			
4-Hybrid			
5-Iron			
6-Iron			
7-Iron			
8-Iron			
9-Iron			
PW			
GW			
SW			
LW			

Notes about this Course

Notes about my Performance

GAME SCORES

Course:

| Date: | Tee Off Time: |

Handicap:

Par:

Yardage:

Slope:

Rating:

Weather

Conditions:

Temperature:

Wind:

Casual

Competition

9 Holes

18 Holes

Players

Front 9

	1	2	3	4	5	6	7	8	9	TOTAL	GRAND TOTAL
PAR											
SCORE											
TEE BOX											
YARDAGE											
FW											
GIRs											
U&D											
PUTTS											
PENALTIES											

Back 9

	1	2	3	4	5	6	7	8	9	TOTAL	GRAND TOTAL
PAR											
SCORE											
TEE BOX											
YARDAGE											
FW											
GIRs											
U&D											
PUTTS											
PENALTIES											

My Score   Birdies   Doubles+   3-Putts+

Total Pars   Bogeys   Triples+   Penalties

MY YARDAGES

Date:

CLUB	HEAD WIND	TAIL WIND	NO WIND
Driver			
3-Wood			
3-Hybrid			
4-Hybrid			
5-Iron			
6-Iron			
7-Iron			
8-Iron			
9-Iron			
PW			
GW			
SW			
LW			

Notes about this Course

_____

_____

_____

_____

_____

_____

_____

Notes about my Performance

_____

_____

_____

_____

_____

_____

_____

_____

_____

_____

Notes from the 19th Hole

GAME SCORES

Course:

Date: Tee Off Time:

Weather

Conditions:

Temperature:

Wind:

Handicap:

Par:

Yardage:

Slope:

Rating:

Casual

Competition

9 Holes

18 Holes

Players

Front 9

	1	2	3	4	5	6	7	8	9	TOTAL	GRAND TOTAL
PAR											
SCORE											
TEE BOX											
YARDAGE											
FW											
GIRs											
U&D											
PUTTS											
PENALTIES											

Back 9

	1	2	3	4	5	6	7	8	9	TOTAL	GRAND TOTAL
PAR											
SCORE											
TEE BOX											
YARDAGE											
FW											
GIRs											
U&D											
PUTTS											
PENALTIES											

My Score   Birdies   Doubles+   3-Putts+

Total Pars   Bogeys   Triples+   Penalties

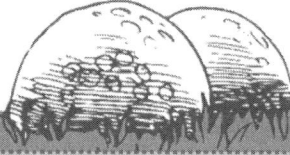

MY YARDAGES

Date:

CLUB	HEAD WIND	TAIL WIND	NO WIND
Driver			
3-Wood			
3-Hybrid			
4-Hybrid			
5-Iron			
6-Iron			
7-Iron			
8-Iron			
9-Iron			
PW			
GW			
SW			
LW			

Notes about this Course

Notes about my Performance

Notes from the 19th Hole

HANDICAP
PROGRESSION

MY TARGETS

Current Handicap

Target Handicap

Current Date:

Date Achieved:

Current Averages		Target Averages	
Fairways Hit		Fairways Hit	
GIRs		GIRs	
Up & Downs		Up & Downs	
3-Putts		3-Putts	
No./Putts		No./Putts	
Penalties		Penalties	
Average Score		Target Score	

AREAS FOR IMPROVEMENT

NOTES ON PROGRESS

MY TARGETS

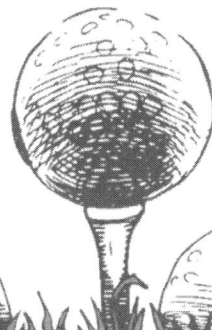

Current Handicap

Target Handicap

Current Date:

Date Achieved:

Current Averages

Fairways Hit	
GIRs	
Up & Downs	
3-Putts	
No./Putts	
Penalties	
Average Score	

Target Averages

Fairways Hit	
GIRs	
Up & Downs	
3-Putts	
No./Putts	
Penalties	
Target Score	

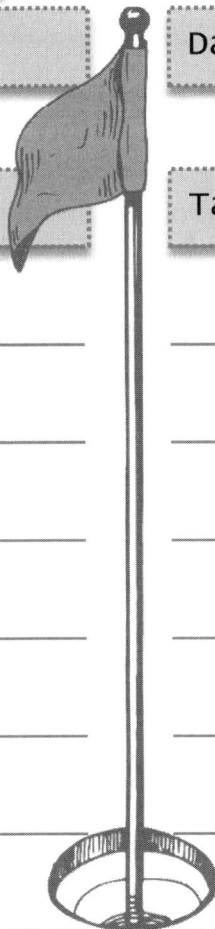

AREAS FOR IMPROVEMENT

MY TARGETS

Current Handicap

Target Handicap

Current Date:

Date Achieved:

Current Averages		Target Averages	
Fairways Hit		Fairways Hit	
GIRs		GIRs	
Up & Downs		Up & Downs	
3-Putts		3-Putts	
No./Putts		No./Putts	
Penalties		Penalties	
Average Score		Target Score	

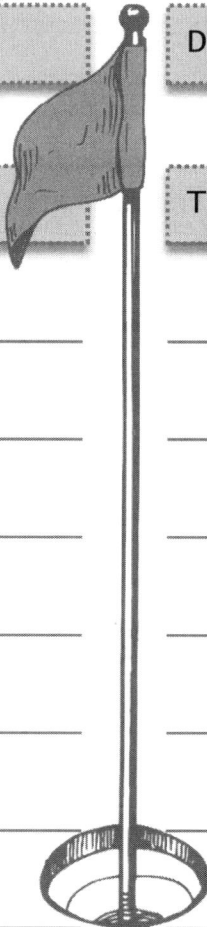

NOTES ON PROGRESS

MY
TARGETS

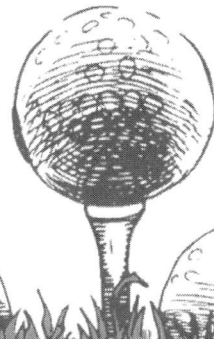

Current
Handicap

Target
Handicap

Current Date:

Date Achieved:

Current Averages

Target Averages

Current		Target	
Fairways Hit		Fairways Hit	
GIRs		GIRs	
Up & Downs		Up & Downs	
3-Putts		3-Putts	
No./Putts		No./Putts	
Penalties		Penalties	
Average Score		Target Score	

AREAS FOR IMPROVEMENT

NOTES ON PROGRESS

GOLF
TOURNAMENTS
&
EVENTS

TOURNAMENT TRACKER

Date	Tournament	Course	Entry Fee	Entry Closing Date	Entered ✓

TOURNAMENT TRACKER

Date	Tournament	Course	Entry Fee	Entry Closing Date	Entered ✓

EVENT STATS

Event: _____

Course: _____

Date: _____ **Tee Off Time:** _____

Entry Fee: _____ **Prize:** _____

 # In Field

Position Finished

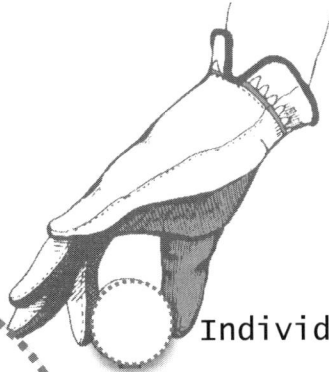

Individual

Four Ball

9 Holes

18 Holes

Yardage: _____

Slope: _____

Rating: _____

Weather

Conditions: _____

Temperature: _____

Wind: _____

Players

_____

_____

_____

_____

Scores and Leaderboard

Round	1	2	3	4
Score				
Finished				
TOTAL SCORE				

EVENT STATS

Event: _____

Course: _____

Date: _____ **Tee Off Time:** _____

Entry Fee: _____ **Prize:** _____

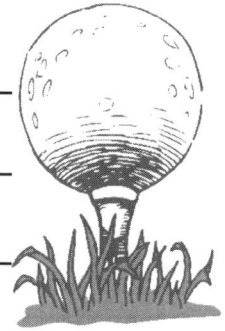

 # In Field

Position Finished

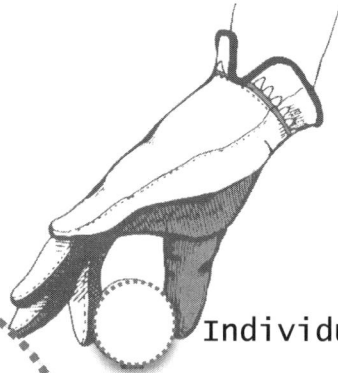

Yardage: _____

Slope: _____

Rating: _____

○ Individual

○ Four Ball

○ 9 Holes

○ 18 Holes

Weather

Conditions: _____

Temperature: _____

Wind: _____

Players

_____

_____

_____

Scores and Leaderboard

Round	1	2	3	4
Score				
Finished				
TOTAL SCORE				

EVENT STATS

Event: _____

Course: _____

Date: _____ **Tee Off Time:** _____

Entry Fee: _____ **Prize:** _____

( ) **# In Field**

Position Finished ( )

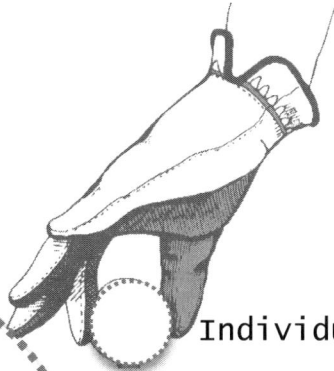

Individual ( )

Four Ball ( )

9 Holes ( )

18 Holes ( )

Yardage:
_____

Slope:
_____

Rating:
_____

Weather

Conditions:
_____

Temperature:
_____

Wind:
_____

Players

_____

_____

_____

_____

Scores and Leaderboard

Round	1	2	3	4
Score				
Finished				
TOTAL SCORE				

EVENT STATS

Event: _____

Course: _____

Date: _____ **Tee Off Time:** _____

Entry Fee: _____ **Prize:** _____

 # In Field

Position Finished

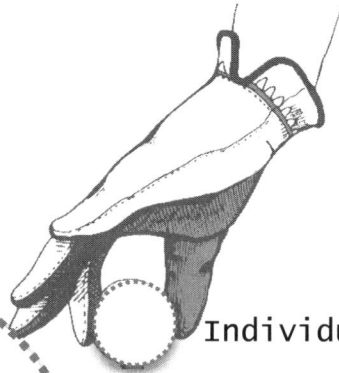

Individual

Four Ball

9 Holes

18 Holes

Yardage: _____

Slope: _____

Rating: _____

Weather

Conditions: _____

Temperature: _____

Wind: _____

Players

_____

_____

_____

_____

Scores and Leaderboard

Round	1	2	3	4
Score				
Finished				
TOTAL SCORE				

EVENT STATS

Event: _____

Course: _____

Date: _____ **Tee Off Time:** _____

Entry Fee: _____ **Prize:** _____

In Field

Position Finished

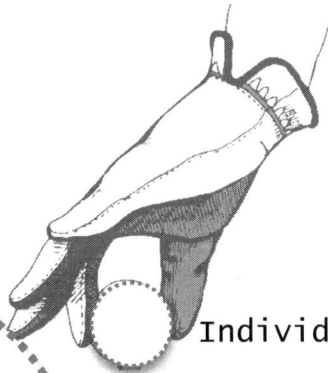

Individual

Four Ball

9 Holes

18 Holes

Yardage: _____

Slope: _____

Rating: _____

Weather Conditions: _____

Temperature: _____

Wind: _____

Players

_____

_____

_____

_____

Scores and Leaderboard

Round	1	2	3	4
Score				
Finished				
TOTAL SCORE				

EVENT STATS

Event: _____

Course: _____

Date: _____ **Tee Off Time:** _____

Entry Fee: _____ **Prize:** _____

 # In Field

Position Finished

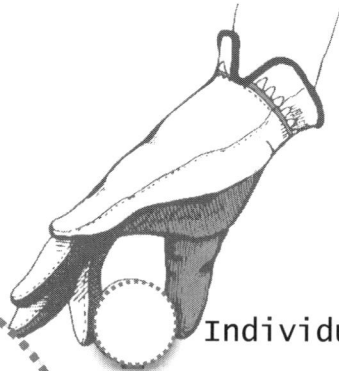

Yardage: _____

Slope: _____

Rating: _____

○ Individual

○ Four Ball

○ 9 Holes

○ 18 Holes

Weather

Conditions: _____

Temperature: _____

Wind: _____

Players

_____

_____

_____

_____

Scores and Leaderboard

Round	1	2	3	4
Score				
Finished				
TOTAL SCORE				

GOLFING
FINANCES

FINANCE

Date	Details	Budget		Actual	
	Clothing				
	Equipment				
	Tournaments				
	Sponsorships				
	19th Hole				

FINANCE

Date	Details	Budget		Actual	

FINANCE

Date	Details	Budget		Actual	

Golfing Thoughts & Reminders...

Golfing Thoughts & Reminders...

Golfing Thoughts & Reminders...

Printed in Great Britain
by Amazon